This book is dedicated to my empaths,
The ones who feel all of life intensely,
The ones who sense the shift in another's voice and energy,
The ones who go to sleep exhausted at night after a long day of carrying everyone's pain.
The ones who feel so deeply hurt by the state of the world.
This is for my true empaths,
The ones who were brought here to feel too much,
You are not too much, nor are you too little,
You are not brittle,
Your sensitivity is not here for you to break apart.
But break open the hearts of those who might have forgotten about their deep, wild and honest emotions,
Their longings and their yearnings to reunite with the Divine.
This is for my true empaths,
Your sensitivity is your greatest weapon,
Your greatest superpower,
It is your antenna, your psychic sense,
To uncover a world beyond this one.
So,
Feel too much.
Be too much.
And know, you have been gifted with the ability to bridge the old with the new and birth new realities
I love you, I know you see me. I see you too.

ABOUT THE BOOK

There are many paths to experiencing unconditional, divine and eternal love.

There are many ways for revelations to come through.

Poetry has been a medium for me to express some of my most mystical experiences. Yet, none of these poems can ever do them justice.

The experiences themselves are unexplainable and cannot be put into words and yet, I have tried to capture them in what I have written.

My journey with poetry started with writing poems about the mind. The mind is where my whole spiritual journey began. Having a busy mind full of thoughts, I found peace in my meditation practice. There were moments I felt my mind grow louder in silence, and I could no longer hear the million thoughts racing constantly. Catching a glimpse of the spaces in between my thoughts, I started to discover my formlessness, eternity and divinity.

This is when the nature of my poetry changed. I became fascinated by mysticism. I fell in love with a God of my own understanding, all over again. I had fallen from grace in my late teens, and stopped believing in any form of Higher Power. Through energy healing, meditation and movement practices, I found myself so immersed in the present moment, I would end up in tears. Tears of joy. Heart full of gratitude. The love I have experienced and continue to experience in these moments of oneness happened not by seeking out for them, but by being. Existing. Connecting. Merging. My connection to a Higher Power has only grown more in intensity and I feel closer to God today, than ever before.

This leads to the final part where love was further discovered in union. In relationships. The length of them matter far less than their impact. The nature of these experiences allowed me to discover that love is not found in others, but has been within me all along. The love I have for myself has grown with each and every rapture. Some of these stories are personal to me. However, as a poet and writer, I like to share stories. Stories from people I have encountered. Stories of people I have imagined. Made up stories. True stories. Being an attentive and empathetic listener has allowed me to understand relationships more deeply.

"Heaven rings in my ears" is a compilation of five years' worth of scribbling notes in my journal and phone. You will notice a change in voice, in tone, in style, and in rhythm. As I myself have grown and transformed over the years, I discovered my ever-changing nature as well as my true essence.

I try to explain this connection I feel with the Divine, with God, with the Universe in so many ways throughout these poems and I hope I am able to convey some of its essence to you.

We may have lost sight of heaven. We may have fallen from grace. We may seek for answers about who we are, what we are meant to do and who we are meant to do it with.

Hopefully through reading these poems, you can begin to hear heaven whispering in your ears, like it has been doing in mine.

We do not find peace, we cultivate peace. We learn to make peace with our non-peace.

We do not need to die to reach heaven. We are in heaven. When we tap into the space of silence and find stillness within.

God exists within each and everyone of us. Everywhere. All the time.

May your beingness bring joy and healing to the world.

May you spend your life sharing your authentic self with others.

May you be in union with your true nature and find the courage within to overcome any of your fears.

May you flood yourself and others with love.

From my heart to yours,

Maria

NEW BEGINNINGS

It's always a little overwhelming. Opening a new blank page of a notebook.
"How do I start? Where will the story go? What if what I write isn't as good as what has already been written?"
The blank page of a notebook is like the beginning of a new day.
"How do I start? Where will my day go? What if today isn't as good as yesterday?"
The blank page of a notebook is like the beginning of a new chapter in life.
"How will it start? Where will this chapter take me? What if this story isn't as thrilling as the previous one?"
The beginning of a blank page, of a new day, of a new chapter presents gifts left unopened, unexplored, untouched.
It also presents challenges to overcome, to break through, to surrender.
The pathways are limitless, options endless.
Yet, you are the one holding the pen.
How tightly are you gripping on to it, unable to hear the whispering in your ear.
"Go this way, trust me" I hear
"Go ahead, write this" it tells me
When I do pay attention, the words on the page come alive
The day is splashed with new colors and visions
The current chapter becomes the only chapter that matters
Yes, you are holding the pen, and the notebook
How, what and when you decide to write is up to whether or not you are listening to the song sung to you from beyond
You are free in the choices you make
Yet, if you can trust that the sweet, loving song sung for you is greater than the one your fearful ones screams from the rooftops,
Your life will resemble a masterpiece
And you my dear, will know peace.

"And that is how you become the writer of a million stories but the author of none."

TABLE OF CONTENTS

THE MIND

Your mind can either be your greatest ally, or your worst enemy.
It all depends on the seeds you have been planting in the garden of your mind.
It is reliant on whether you have cut the weeds off from the root so you can free yourself and be your Self.

To rewire the mind is perhaps one of the greatest contributions a human being can do to make this world a better place. Your thoughts carry weight. They can make you feel light or heavy, strong or weak, healthy or sick. Your thoughts influence the collective consciousness, whether you are aware of their impact.

Having experienced depression in my teenage years, I discovered tools to help steady the fluctuations of my mind. For over six years, I have either started my mornings with a yoga or meditation practice which have provided much relief, revelation and growth. These poems are written in those moments of clarity where my pen would take over and I had no control over what came through.

May our minds be free from our burdensome thoughts,
May our thoughts bring healing to ourselves and the world,
May they contribute to the evolution of our planet and the birth of a new world.

Unlearning

You don't know you need healing, until you start the process
You don't know your thoughts or feelings, unless you pay attention to them when they arise
You don't know another's story, until you listen to them speak
You don't know your True Self's magnificence, unless you experience it
You don't know that you don't know until you realise this journey is the undoing of all that you believed you knew

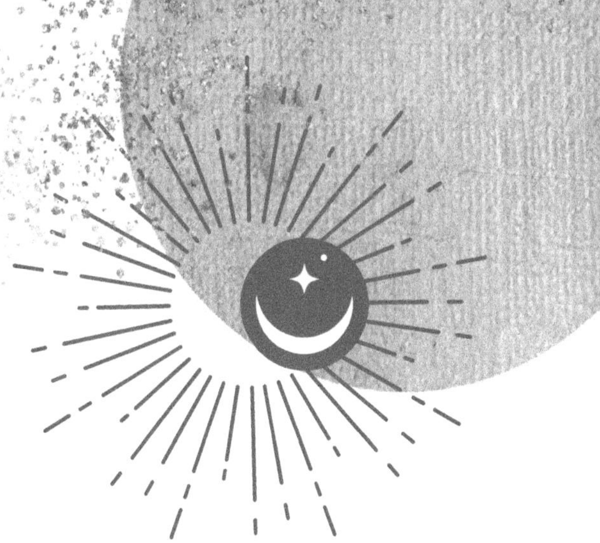

People pleaser

All my life I tried to please, not because I am a tease,
but because I wanted others to feel at ease
I remained silent and abiding
hiding
behind my splendor in terror
In trying to mold myself into everything I am not,
I told myself once and for all that it was enough!
It was time to stop apologizing
and be uncompromising
about who I am and what I want
My purpose is to be of service
and to bring light to the dark night
With my will and might,
I will take flight
and delight with no end in sight

Inside the head of a mad woman

Inside the head of a mad women

You'll find her bathing in a bath of her own sorrows

Buried under the weight of her burdens

Talking to herself

What are they doing?

Are they having as much fun as they make it seem?

Is fame really the end game?

Is that what we're all striving for?

Recognise me

Hear me

See me

Love

Me

Pick

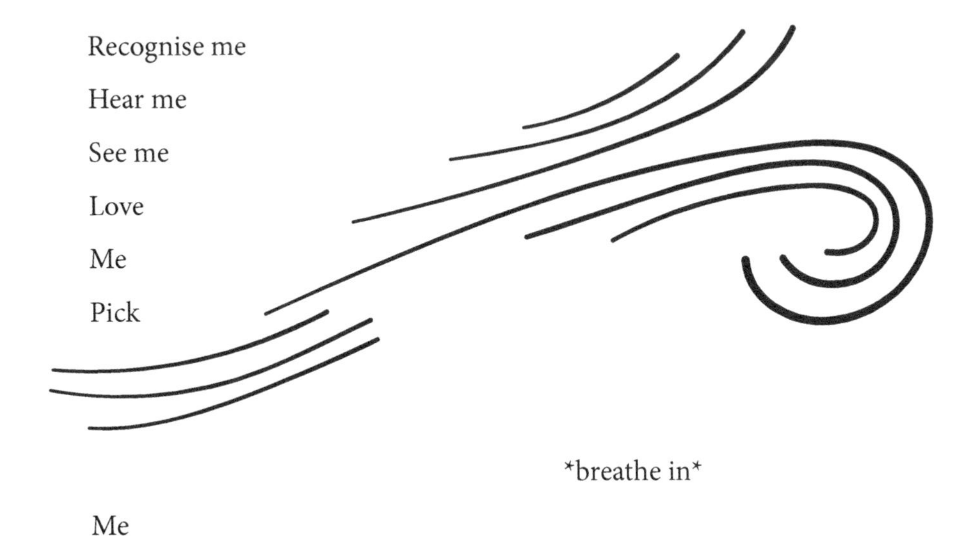

breathe in

Me

breathe out

The longest war

The longest war is the one we wage on ourselves against ourselves

It is the most common war that has ever been had
The one where the enemy is always yourself
The one where your soul burns in a hell that is self-made
The one where there are no winners

There is only yourself tainted and almost bled to death
Why does one choose to be at war with oneself?
Causing suffering not only to the soul that resides within your body, but those around you too

Why does one not see their own light like they do of others?

Why does one listen to the voices of evil and darkness and choose to ignore the voices of reason and wisdom?

The war ends only when we surrender our arms

Turn up our palms

Open our hearts

Rise above our minds

Master peace

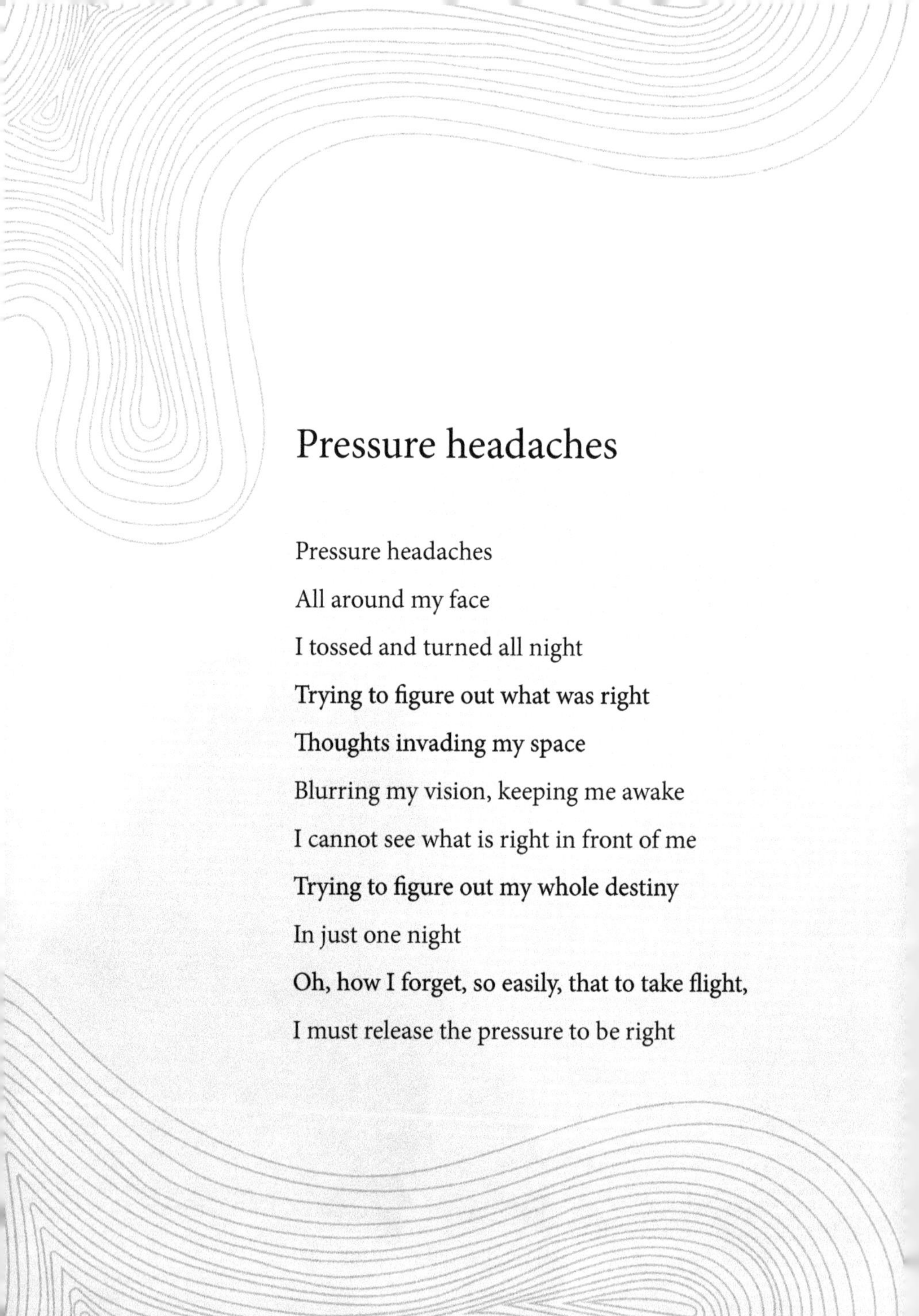

Pressure headaches

Pressure headaches

All around my face

I tossed and turned all night

Trying to figure out what was right

Thoughts invading my space

Blurring my vision, keeping me awake

I cannot see what is right in front of me

Trying to figure out my whole destiny

In just one night

Oh, how I forget, so easily, that to take flight,

I must release the pressure to be right

Meditate

The more thoughts you have in your mind,

The less space there is for you to come up with creative ideas

The more thoughts you have in your mind,

The less time you spend checking in with your heart's desires

The more thoughts you have in your mind,

The less risks you take

Everything becomes calculated

Pre prepared

Planned

Micromanaged

Micro analysed

Losing touch with reality, with your own body

And your true longing

Space

The space of silence in my mind allows for greater healing of
the body and soul
It allows for a deeper kind of healing
One that involves energetic clearing

The space of silence allows for creativity to flow in
It enhances my intuition and senses
It bring me back to the here and now
Without all the heavy luggages I have accumulated over the
years
It brings me back home remembering again " I am whole"

The space of silence allows for divine connection,
healing and love to fill up my entire being

My eyes brighten , I see the world differently
When I look at my inner world from a loving and
compassionate perspective, I cannot help but do the same in
the external one

However, the space of silence in my mind gets noisy throughout the day
The entertainment it plays throughout, like an old CD or DVD on replay
Thoughts, unconscious habits, behaviours, patterns, play out
In the blink of the eye, I have lost this connection

It is not a good versus bad
It just is
It is the ebb and flow that is life
It is the natural rhythm and cycle we all belong to

And so,
In those moments where my mind is still and silent
I cherish them and savour them as much as I can
Knowing that it is impermanent
and it is the fleetingness of it all that makes me even more grateful
For the next moment, who knows who I will greet at the door?

With or Without

I am whole, with or without

With or without the things I identify myself as

With or without the things I identify to

With or without external approval or validation

I am whole, always, with or without

Wholeness and holiness flow within me all times, with or without my realisation

Be Free

Be free. Be free.

Be free of what anyone thinks, including yourself

Wasting time on what others are thinking, is a thought in itself

It is an experience within yourself

It it not reality

An assumption at best

Even if you were a mind reader

Even if you are able to catch the thoughts of another,

Be free from it

It is simply a projection of their own judgements towards themselves

Mantras on safety

I am safe to be

I am safe to be me

I am safe to be expressive

I am safe to be weird and funny

witty and argumentative

I am safe to embody this body

I am safe in my own skin

I am safe. I am safe. I am safe.

And so, it is

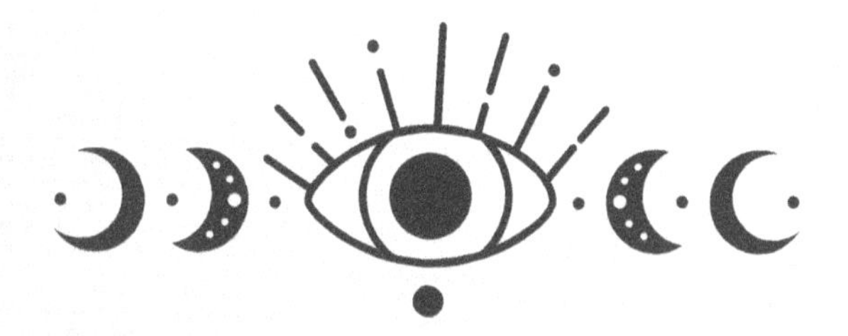

Home buddy

Get back into your body again

It is safe for you to live in this body

This body is a safe body

This body is a home buddy

It isn't where you leave your cigarette buds

It is where you live

Nourish it

Nurture it

Love it

Embuddy it

On rest

I allow myself to rest

To release the wrestle between me and the present moment

Rest is not for the wicked

It is for the wise

Your ticket home

There is no separation between your pain and your purpose

Where you once were hurt, or brought down to your knees,

because life got too hard, too messy, too complicated,

There is a reason

To bring you closer to your truth, to your reason for being here

Whether it is to awaken you spiritually or to get back into your body

Do not bypass the pain

Learn from it, grow through it

Let it be your ticket back home

For once you return and let your soul embody its impermanent but beautiful home, you will come to realise

The darkness and light are all one and the same

That your purpose can be found in your pain

“To be reborn, one has to die before dying”

Maybe, as I become anew, there is a period of grief to all that I knew
A period of darkness as I my way through

Maybe, I am still grieving the death of my old self
Grasping on to all that is not mine
Making it harder to find the true gold mine

Losing myself in the memories of the past
Trying to make them last
Although not all of them were a blast

Maybe as I become anew, there is a period of
grief to all that I knew
And saying goodbye is never easy, but how am I ever meant
to fly if I do not die, first?

Loose & Natural

It's okay for me to let go of my expectations

It's okay that I don't have a timeline for when things will happen for me

I'll empty myself until I fill myself with the whole Universe

Creating the perfect recipe for an inner explosion

My own sort of Big Bang

I'll create the world I want to live in

I'm okay not knowing what comes next

I'm okay with taking it day by day

I'm okay not being okay with it sometimes

I'll surrender more whenever I feel my grip tightening or when my belly knots up

How can the energy flow properly when I'm holding on too tightly?

Loose and natural. Loose and natural. I want to be loose and natural

Let it be

Let it go

Let it flow

Let it grow

Let it die

Be reborn

Shadows

She's fighting
Her shadows
Her shadows
She's fighting her demons
Every day

She's distraught and angry
She's physically in pain

Earth's biggest challenge is humanity
The vibrations of fear, greed, and hate

Her biggest obstacles are drama, mama
Get wiser
Grow taller
Your bones will ache
Every inch of you will hurt
To remind you of the pain of Mother Earth

To hold on or to let go?

Stop holding on to a story that does not want to be written

Stop holding on to a thought that brings you no joy

Stop holding on to a feeling that rarely ever lasts

Stop holding on to your breath to not drop dead

Stop holding on to shame and do not blame another for what you have done to yourself

Stop for a moment
Drop into the moment

Be still

Breathe forever

Antics of the mind

How many deaths do you think this sea has seen?

It seems at peace now

But does anything ever last forever?

Scribbling down my thoughts

I have to put them down somewhere

How will I know the true antics of the mind if I don't follow

the stream of thoughts enter?

Battles of the Egos

And you're still here, after all this time

You're still here, after all this pain

No matter what they do

You remain

No matter how they do it

You stand in the light of God

And you're still here, after all this time

Your roots grow deeper

After all this time

Do you not know yet?

The truth always comes out

The lies never win

You cannot love with deceit

Deception is for the ones who cannot see that what is happening is a human tragedy

If we were to travel back in time,

We would always find injustices happen when we do not treat a human life as a human life,

Fear reigns when we don't peel off the layers back to oneness

And you're still here, after all this time
You're still here, after all this pain

Your existence is persistence

You've prayed to the Lord up above and your dark path is being lit up again

Change doesn't happen simultaneously
All at once
Overnight

To heal the wound,
You must treat the disease

Fighting is not what this journey is all about
Our life's work has always been about pouring our love into action

Remember to recognise one another, like you would want to be recognised
Treat one another, like you would want to be treated
Love one another, like you would want to be loved

Stormy Weather

I know why storms are followed by rain
Why when I blow up in anger, I cry
I know I can hurt others with my words
That my tongue can cut through steel
I know I am not always kind nor do I claim to be
I can see my ancestors dancing in the sea
Reminding me of where I will one day be
A wave crashing against a stone
Sand underneath my children's feet

It is so hard to outgrow where you've grown
And to move somewhere yet unknown
But it is far harder to keep knocking on old doors
Waiting for an apology you will never receive

Oh, my child, I am so sorry you have been so hurt
I do wish you otherwise
If they had been truly wise, they would have
brushed your hair instead of bashing your head

Oh child, I know how much your heart hurts
And how your scars are taking too long to heal
I know you're trying your best to pass this test, to
not fail at being a good child, faithful friend, and
eternal lover

I know your heart and how it beats
For I am the One who created the sun and the heat

An Outlier

My mind wanders a lot sometimes

My heart has been broken one too many times

And I am tired of being too sweet, too nice, too gentle

My lips are not just capable of uttering sweet, sweet nothings

My words are not always wrapped in love

Sometimes,

Sometimes I like the feeling of not listening to you, of talking back, of walking away

I guess sometimes you just have to write a ton of shit for something good to come out

What is worthy? What isn't? Why are some sentences so much better than others?

Why do you get tell me that my art isn't art?

Or that my poetry isn't poetry?

I am mad

I am mad

At the many men of the world

I am mad at the diseases we have created

I am mad at myself

For falling into the same traps again and again thinking the outcome will be different

I don't want to walk down this road anymore
I want to pave my own

I don't want to be used anymore
Abused any longer

I am tired of you flipping your mind like the flip of a switch

I don't care that none of this makes any sense
I don't care that my poetry isn't beautiful and makes you quite uncomfortable

I don't want to be sweet or easy to digest
I want you to choke a little while reading my words
It seems all of us become nicer when we are closer to death anyway

A pinch of patience

A pinch of patience, added to a body of water

The turbulence of my mind settled

It was not that the world around me stopped spinning

It was not that I had all of the answers figured out

Life was continuously flowing like a river

I just decided to keep my heart open to Love,

I allowed for that to be the fragrance I wear,

Breakthroughs happen when a crack happens from the inside

New life begins when you choose to let go

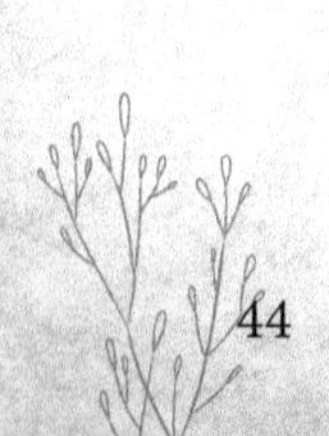

Be at peace

To experience inner peace,

You have to be at peace

With your non-peace

WONDER

In our heads too much, in our bodies too little

We seek for extremes in everything:

In love, in food, in drugs, in pleasure and even in pain

In our heads too often, we forget to be playful, to be curious, to be, to exist,

We move too often, listen too little,

We worry instead of wonder how miraculous our existence really is

How temporary all of life is and yet how eternity can be glimpsed at each moment of each day

The Stairway to Heaven

Each day, each moment, each second, I have the choice to
become aware of the space my mind dips into
Some moments, I slip into fearful spaces
Spaces where I'm in the wild jungle in the middle of the night
no end in sight
or drowning in the depths of the ocean flooding my body
with terror
Some moments I'm climbing the ladder towards heaven
There are no rails
Around me,
Only air,
There is no fear as I climb towards the high skies
My imagination runs wild and I let it, as long as it's running
towards the stairway of heaven
Confidently putting one foot in front of the other, trusting I
won't fall when I have love in my heart
Trusting the clouds will let me rest when I need to take a
break
Remembering heaven is all around me and I am held in the
hands of God, even when I don't know it
My imagination runs wilds and I let it, as long as it's running
towards the stairway of heaven

Miraculous Mornings

Every morning, I wake up

My eyes open after a night in slumber

There is so much to see outside my window. The sunrise. The birds flying. The clouds drifting.

So why do I scroll through my phone, tiring my eyes when I've barely noticed the wonders of this new and gifted day?

I take the morning light for granted. I just expect to be alive. I barely noticed the big little moments that make each day up.

I jump out of bed barely acknowledging the Earth below my feet.
I rush.

I rush. I rush. I rush. To get ready. To eat. To get through the door and out into the jungle of this wild, wild city.

Why am I more concerned with my labor and my chores?
Why do I believe that what I do is who I am?

I move fast. I run. In the opposite direction of the sun. I take no notes of this new dawn. I hear nothing but the thoughts in my own head.

And then I wonder, why am I so drained? Why am I feeling so tired?
I started my day without a prayer. Without any appreciation and gratitude.

And so now, I pause. To still my mind so it can notice. What is true and real and what isn't.

I pray for this brand new day. I feel the ground below my feet.
I no longer jump out of bed. I eat in silence. I play music while I get ready. I meditate. I write. I sing and hum a song when my eyes first open. I stop checking my phone and I start looking outside.
I see people. Moving fast. The cars going up and down the street.

But I, I'll move slow in the early morning. I don't want to miss out on the miracle of a brand new day.

Home again

My thinking mind wants to be in control

Another part of me wants to slow it down

It wants to absorb it all: the sounds of the waterfalls, the birds chirping

I want to take in all the vibrant colors and I want to notice the yellow leaves falling on the ground

Observing movement in stillness, stillness in movement

I soften my gaze to soften my thinking mind

I soften the grip I have on my pen to notice the brush of the ink and how it caresses the paper gently

I remember fond memories from long ago, holding them close to my heart

The wind is picking up, the light is changing

The leaves on the trees moving quicker, and yet here I am

Noticing all the yellow leaves falling

With moments of wonder about what my futures holds

With moments of pure awareness, I am not sure where it all ends and begins

Nature, myself, time

How inspiring that I get to be a witness of this moment
How grateful I am to hear the birds sing, see the light change, feel the wind blowing my hair again, to smell the freshness of green grass
To touch this pen
How simple these actions are and yet how rarely do I notice them in their entirety

Being present that there is no separation between me and the experience
There is no separation between me and the moment

Tears are filling my eyes up; it feels good to touch my own beating heart again
Tears are rolling down my face, I taste it on my tongue, how thirsty have I been for my own love?

A lady passes me by with a bucket of flowers on her head
We exchanged a smile and greeting
How long have I waited to finally see myself in others and others in myself?

My arms are interlaced around my legs, I have waited so long to feel the depth of my own love

It feels good to be home again

The pandemic

"And where do you think you're going?" - the World asked of me

Have you lost your head, believing you can get ahead?

Go within. Go without. Stop having so much doubt!

You're running around restlessly, like a restless sea

This time may not be the norm, but it has the ability to transform

Forced to stay still instead, I realised that being dead was holding my breath

Thinking that I had somewhere to go, because I believed where I was is a No

I took my time and noticed that all our lives went by unnoticed

Living completely unaware, the Truth declared:

"The present moment is all there and this time

You have to bear it"

Worthy of love

There are times I question,

"Am I even worthy of being held? Of being loved by You?"

It may sound silly, but sometimes I don't feel like I deserve it

I learned along the way that I had to be a certain way

I had to do certain things to feel worthy,

My hair needed to be combed

My face and eyes had to be clear

Messiness was not deemed of being loved

And oh my, how messy I've been

How unclear some of my thoughts were

How my actions weren't always pure and yet

You come to me with the cure

Really?

You still love this mess?

Tears rolling down my face, I hear a whisper near my ear,

"Love is always here, even if you are not

Love is always here

Present

Unconditional

Overflowing

Even when you don't recognize it

All you ever need to remember is that the source of

life is love

The source of life is love and to love you are destined

to return"

The Mystery of Life

"Why am I here?
You asked yourself at some point in life

"What does it mean to be alive? How did this all happen?
Where do I go when I die?"

There are theories,
Philosophies,
Religious books,
Accounts from people who have seen the light,
Giving us hope,
There might be an afterlife, after all

People before us have come and gone
And we too, will go

The question of life,
The question of life before birth,
The question of life after death,

I realise now I have not asked the right questions.

How different would my answers be, if I asked:

"How can I live for the moment and not in the past or future?

How can I take all this in and grow and learn and be open to all possibilities?

Can I see the magic in the simplest yet most intricate things like a flower or the sunlight?"

If we look at the time span of our planet, we all make a very short appearance

And so, it begs me to ask this last question:

"How can I live each day as if it were my first?"

You are not alone

A door opens,

I enter alone

I am not sure where I am heading

I am a little afraid

Everything is dark and I cannot find the light switch

I am looking for why I am here, am I being punished?

I am not sure

All I know is

I am in the Unknown and I do not seem at peace with it

I do not know where I am going or where I am heading

"Invite faith in" I hear

"Let God enter the room"

Now the lights are on again, I did not even have to look for the switch

Everything is so bright; it is almost blinding

I cannot see so well either

I ask for God to dim the lights a little

The lights are readjusted

My eyes are more settled

And I hear once more,

“

the right
amount of darkness is
necessary to be embraced by the light,
your struggles are not your struggles, they
are your path to Enlightenment
if only you let
God enter
the room

”

Life is a series

Life is a series of unexpected events

Some we cannot comprehend

They blow us out of the park

Given their intensity and their depth

"Why this? Why us?" we often ask ourselves when an external event happens beyond our comprehension

The pain is so deep, the cuts take forever to heal

We have so much difficulty accepting the unacceptable

"What have I done to deserve this?" we ask the Power above us hopelessly

Nothing. You have nothing to deserve this. This is not a test

Your worthiness is not dependent on external events

All that is required in this moment is unwavering faith in the Divine plan laid out before you

All that is ever asked from you is your undivided presence

What happens if I lose my head?

If I lose my head,
Just for a moment,

What would happen?
Would I lose sight of what is right?

If I lose my head,
And tap into my heart
Just for a moment

What would happen?
Would I have a fright?

If I lose my head,
Just for a moment
Would I dance differently?

If I lose my head,
Would I love differently?

If I lose my head,

Would I choose you over me?

No that can't be

That can't be

If I lose my head,

I would be free

If I lose my head

I would be me

If I lose my head

I will see You

In everything

In every being

Everywhere

Your thoughts are a prayer

What if you imagined your thoughts to be a prayer?

How much more aware would you be of what you said to yourself?

How much more careful would you be of what you said about others?

How much more creative would you be if you knew you could create your life?

How much more loving would you be to yourself and to others?

What would you utter?

THE DIVINE

Once the mind is clearer and you have finally let go of who you think you are, you tap into a realm that most of us have lost sight of. The realm of the divine. The realm of an everlasting, ever flowing, ever giving energy of love and healing. The presence of God is not just found in churches, temples, mosques, synagogues and temples. The presence of God is found in all moments of the day. It is living, alive, pulsating in every cell of your body. This power is in me, just as is it in you. It is in the so called "enemy", just as much as it is in your mother. It is the Source. Source of strength. Source of courage. Source of my soul. It is so much greater and grandeur than we can gather and comprehend.

This chapter evokes the encounters I have had with the Divine. These moments of union with the Infinite have been nothing short of miraculous, healing and transformational.

The Journey

And the journey

to the Self is really

Just another way of saying

It is a journey

Towards

God

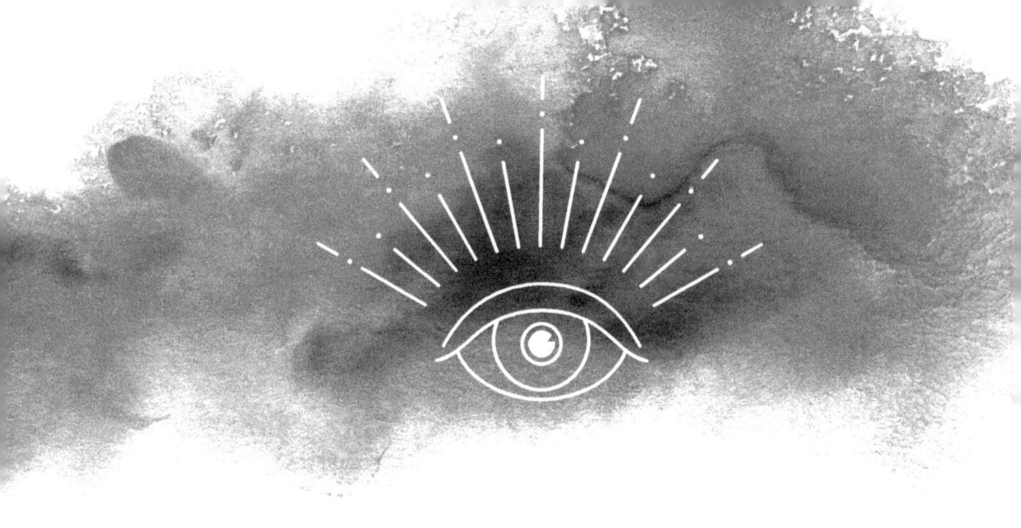

Look Up

We try to create our lives but who best to help us than the One who created Worlds?
We try to change our past but who best to heal it than the One who renews us every day?
We try to modify ourselves but who best to accept us than the One who formed us?

Shake it off

Why do we let life's experiences harden us?

Why do we let heartbreak, break us?

Why do we become so sour and tangy?

Why do we carry the weight of our life experiences on our shoulders?

Let go of what no longer serves you

Return to that vibrant self

Serve the world from a place of love instead of fear

Feel the love of God pouring into your cells at each moment of each day

Remember who you are

It was never about changing who you are

It has always been about

Remembering

And realising

Who you have always been

Unwrap the gift

We believe we desire love, yet we look for it in another
We believe we desire richness, yet we look for it in the material world
We believe we desire security, yet we look for it in a constantly shifting world
We believe we desire passion, yet we pursue passionless projects
We believe we know what we want, yet when we receive it, we desire more, we desire another, we desire different
And when is it exactly that we become satisfied?
When is it that we feel full and fulfilled?
When is it that we recognise our box contains multitude of gifts unwrapped still because we were unaware of their presence?
Unwrap the gift this moment offers you, and you will come to know the Eternal, the Divine, the Infinite

The world's lost it

You know the world's lost it
When love is only ever written about and never experienced

You know the world's lost it
When love is portrayed as a knight in shining armour and not a night sky full of stars

You know the world's lost it
When love is an indoctrination and not a divine devotion to all of life

A fantasy and not a reality

A fairytale and not a revelation

You know the world's lost it
When love is not seen in the unseen
Felt in the unfelt
Heard in the silence

Heaven is light

As you choose to enter the Kingdom,

You must leave your bags at the door,

Heaven is light and even your carry on is heavy.

To feel love, you have to empty.

Empty the bags, empty the mind,

Drop the past and the pain.

Heaven is light and even your carry on is heavy,

The angels are waiting for you now to sip tea,

Are you ready?

To leave your bags at the door and enter the Kingdom, empty?

The Divine lives in All

When you are connected

You find beauty in sitting near your window on an early morning

Basking in the sunlight

And you don't know why

It's so beautiful and overwhelming

Your heart can almost cry of joy

The sun lighting up your body to show you your edges

Giving you a glimpse of what the divine can look like

It looks like you,

It looks like me,

It looks like the trees and the flowers,

The divine can smell like rain and sound like thunder

It lives in All

In Truth and in the opposite of Truth

For if it were to exist in All, it has to take into account its opposite

And so,

That is how you begin to make peace with what you might deem untruthful and ugly

That is how you begin to make peace with the unpeaceable

You recognise

If the divine lives in All, it must live in the opposite of what you have been taught of what is good

right

and light

There is only Oneness

There are as many truths as there are people in the world
But there is only one Truth that is Universal and Eternal
God's silent yet echoing language of love

There are as many perceptions as there are people in the world
But there is only One that sees all always
God's omnipresent yet invisible eyes

There are as many projections as there are experiences in the world
But there is only one that is clear as a sunny day
God's heavenly mind, heart and spirit

Who am I if not loved by You?

The sky is painted with my favourite shades of blue

and all I can do is think of You

You, who fills me up when I run empty

You, who brings me wine when I am thirsty

You, who feeds me Truth when I am hungry

You, who cleanses my eyes from illusions

Drawing me in closer towards You

I have never felt closer to the heavens

Oh You, the All Mighty and divine, my devotion towards You grows each day

Oh You, the Creator, who am I if not loved by You?

Creation

Creation comes from darkness

So why are we so afraid of the dark, when the dark night birthed light?

Creation comes from nothingness

So why are we so afraid of being nothing, when emptiness gave us beingness?

Creation comes from silence

So why are we so afraid of the silence when stillness connects us to source?

Creation comes from explosions

So why are we so afraid when things explode, when outbursts brings in new life?

Safety is delusional

The only comfort you will ever find lies not in your finances or the four walls surrounding you
It sits so deep, no soul could ever cut through it, no event could ever take it away
You may believe your being is in shambles because of all the knots
And not's you have
The carpet may have been rugged from underneath your feet
Forget it my friend, safety is an illusion for the one who has not found God in breath

If you stay or if you go

And my light will not burn out if you stay or if you go

And my laughter will not weaken if you stay or if you go

And my heart will only grow more in love if you stay or if you go

For I am always at one with the One who never leaves

Heaven rings in my ears

It is like they sang heaven in my ears
And love began pouring through my pores

Voices of angels flooding my mind
Evaporating my heavy thoughts into thin air

It is like they sang heaven in my ears
And love began pouring through my pores

The hairs on my body stood up and stood still
For they recognised the notes playing from up above

It is like they sang heaven in my ears
And love began pouring through my pores

My dimmed light was dim no more

Now that love struck a chord on my pierced heart, soothing my melancholic soul

Blessed are those who hear the song sung by the angels

Lucky are those who get to sing it, play it, and be it

It is like they sang heaven in my ears

And love began pouring through my pores

How magnificent is the sound of music when God is present?

Too great and too grand if I dare sing it

Rings of fire

Approach me, child

If you jumped through the rings of fire

You most certainly can walk through the torrents of rain

Now tell me,

How else did you think you would douse it off?

Hazards of Fire need water

Just as much as you need Me

Stormy days

I withered a storm

So big and so grand

And yet, I still found land

I didn't even need to have an atlas

As I found You, at last

Thank God

All these words, I dedicate to You

You have given me a voice, a heart and a beat

I write love notes to You

What else is there one to do?

I'm mesmerised by You

I feel safe writing to You

About You

You never judge nor do You criticise

You never ask me to be who I'm not

You never require me to change

You love me even when I, do not

I write love notes to you

And I cry,

Because the love is strong

And I can never go wrong with You by my side

I find magic even in despair

I manage to love even when love is not there

I turn my anger into art

And I even make peace with the darts that have pierced my sobbing heart

I write love notes to God

Before I close my eyes at night

And as soon as I wake up in the morning

Sometimes they're a simple thank You,

Thank You for shedding light during the dark night

Thank You for being here even when everyone else disappeared

Thank You

Empty your head, find God

When you empty your head of all you wish you could do, be or have
You make room for the invisible to make its way through

Not even your imagination could match with what the Creator can do for you
It cannot fathom the grandness that is possible for you

You can try
Dream big
Trust
In Love's power

Soothe Yourself 

It's okay
It's okay if you took 1 or 100 steps back
It's okay if you thought you had it figured out and it turns out you don't

Soothe yourself. Soothe yourself child. Plant the palm of your hand on your heart. Let it rest there. Let it sit there for a while. Until it grows its own roots. Let yourself smile in memory of what was, and let your heart rejoice in what can still be. It still can. You still can. You're still here.

Soothe yourself.
It's okay if you have nothing under control
It's okay whether you feel dark or light
You are not loved any less. For crying or laughing. For love encompasses it all

Soothe yourself. Let yourself rest in the palms of God's healing hands. Let the plan unravel.

Remember. Remember what you felt. Don't let life's experiences taint black your loving heart

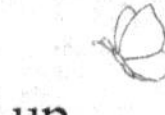

Give it all up

Your attachments

Your desires

Your love,

Give it all, up

Turn your palms up

Turn them

To the skies above your body

Let them float

Let them receive the bountiful

Let your hips sway

Let your soul soar

Let it roar loud

Tilt your head back

Let a sound rip out of your mouth

Until tears roll down your cheeks and land right there on your heart

You have just received

The grace and strength from up above

Let your cells feed off this unconditional love

Catharsis, you are reborn at any time you remember this

All roads lead to the light

All roads lead to the light
How one chooses to walk the path towards the light, back to Source
is a choice

One can choose to pave their own way
One can choose to take the path that has been laid out for them

One can choose the path of least resistance or choose to put many
obstacles on their way
One can choose to do both or none

There are those that will follow the cycles of the moon, the rhythm
of the Universe, the guidance of the stars above
There are those that will dance to the rhythm of their internal drum

There are those that will follow their minds instead of their hearts,
their hearts instead of their minds

There are those that will set fire to their lives to burn it back down to ashes and begin again
Be reborn again. And again. Countless times

There are those that will contemplate it and watch life from the sidelines

All these roads
All these paths
All these journeys one can embark on

Each day a new chance to take a different turn towards the light
Each day a new chance to follow one's calling
Each day a day closer to returning back to the light
How one chooses to walk the path back home is a choice

None are wrong
All lead to the light

Come alive, be present!

And we follow the shadows of the past hoping to arrive to the future of our dreams

If only we appreciated this moment, just as it is
If only we loved ourselves just as we are
If only we trusted the flow of life just as it unfolds
If only we surrendered to the divine just as it should be

We would look at every moment with sparkling eyes
We would love with all of our hearts
We would no longer live in terror but in awe of the gift of being alive

Cross your fingers

Fingers crossed, I say

Things will get better, they say

Pray, I pray,

Things will get better

How about we get better?

At communicating

At handling conflict differently

At looking at all perspectives

At listening

At setting boundaries

At releasing others

Especially the one boundary between God and you,

Should dissolve so you, love

Can evolve

Life makes no mistakes

You may not get it right every time, but you will

Occasionally

Eventually

When it's meant to be

It'll happen and it'll be delightful and I hope you throw your head back in laughter and take it all in

When it does, you better treat it like a miracle because it is and it is divine.

Sweet nectar

The sweetness of doing nothing is

The discovery of everything

The recovery of the body

The uncovering of your True Self

All is One

Everything leads you to where you are right now
And all things are one
And all things are divine

Do not split them into two
The good and the bad
The wrong and the right
The black and the white

Forgiveness is the way through
So is compassion, acceptance, peace and love

Be kinder,
Gentler,
Grow wise,
Rise,
And watch God surprise you at all times.

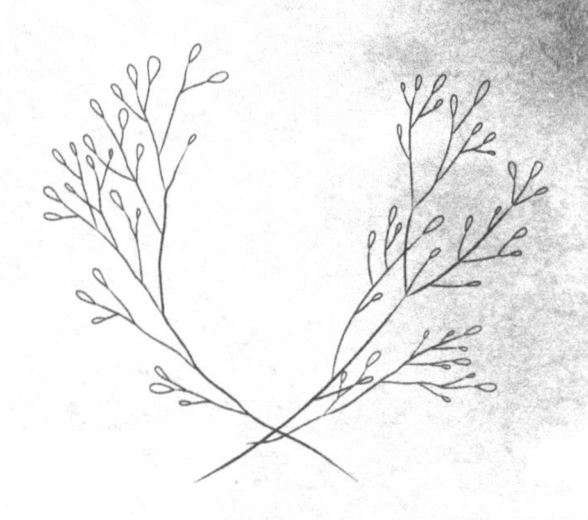

Surrender, sweet child

You try, try, try

To be in control

To be in activity

To be at peace

Yet how can you be at One with it all when you grip on to your belief that you know it all?

Surrender, sweet child, and let me weave for you, with you, the life you are worthy of living

Tiktok

The imaginary clock of time is ticking

It ticks to the sound of birds, of water, of the wind blowing
It ticks to the rhythm of the sun rising, of the sun setting
It ticks to the cycles of the moon
It ticks to the sound of your breath
The rhythm of your heart

The imaginary clock of time is ticking
Its speed determined by the fastness or slowness of your mind chatter
Dependent on your ability to take deep and full breaths
Counting on your willingness to stay present

When you touch this moment right here,
When you raise your arms above your head and look deeply into the vastness and grandness of the deep blue sky
You linger in the eternal space where God lives
You taste, smell, see, hear, touch the sweetness and heavenly presence of the divine

The imaginary clock of time is ticking
You are in front of the unlocked door
Are you ready to enter the kingdom of eternity?

Bedazzle me

A maze is simpler to solve than you,

Even with every twist and turn there's always a way to return

You on the other hand

I enter and I'm amazed

To find no doors

Is it truly open for twenty-four?

Time oh time is an old friend

I've finally made peace with dead ends

You are one mystery not to be solved

Better not to play hide and seek with the dissolved

Divine Drunken Love

We want solutions for the unsolvable

The unknowable

When we do get it,

We don't want it

Or at least not right away

We fight with the present moment

As though it could be anything else than it is

As though by some force of magic you could change it

Oh, but you can,

You see

You have been gifted with free will

You are presented with many options

Love or hate them

They are there for you to pick from

If you trust

If you surrender

If you allow

Life to take you where it needs to take you
Where it needs to break through

You see,
You try to put the sea in a glass of wine
Fine, maybe a whole bottle,
And yet, you still believe you tasted the whole sea
When really, you've only tasted the sea from the wine bottle

And you whine, and you whine, and you whine
About not being able to find a true valentine
You forget,
true love goes beyond the bottle of wine
Into the unsolvable, and unknowable

"This is what I want" - you say
And, I, deliver
You don't know how it is going to be delivered
Only you will get to choose how to respond
Only you will get to choose to redirect
Only you will get to choose to remember
True love goes beyond the bottle

Enough is enough

Was my love not enough?

Not pure enough?

Strong enough?

Healing enough?

Was my way of being too much?

Too sensitive?

Too daring?

Too bold?

Was I too blatant or not blatant enough?

All my life, I've lived between being too much of one thing, too little of another

It always made me wonder if I was not right nor ripe

Like I needed a little bit of salt to my tasteless side

And so, I cried and cried

Until I died, and merged with You

I arose anew, birthed myself and promised to never doubt my worth, and Your word.

MYSTICISM

People around you will keep filling and stuffing your mind with all kinds of things. They will tell you what is and what is not possible. They will logically calculate and share their findings with you. They will dismiss your intuitive knowing. They will doubt you, judge you, outcast you, alienate you.

You can listen to "they" your whole life and not even realize who you are. Or you can become aware. You can remember your own voice, your own truth.

Now, in the logical world we were all born into, sure what they are saying may be partly true. But, is it wholly true? Fully true? Is it holy? Is it divine? Is it magical?

Miracles are possible. For every single one of you. If you want to enter the realm of the mystical, you have to believe in yourself above all else. You have to tune in and tone down any external noise and listen to your own.

You have to believe in yourself and your experiences. You have to trust in your own intuition. Follow your own guidance. You have to walk the path of the heart and sometimes that means walking it on your own for some time. It might mean having to accept that you are the black sheep. The lone wolf. But trust, that as you let go of who you thought you were, you will find your people and they too, will find you.

The road of mysticism is one that the logical mind cannot comprehend. It is one that cannot be understood by everyone. But the heart? The heart knows.

When in doubt about your purpose, your soul's calling, remember this:

I believe in what I do

I believe in how I do it

I believe in the services I bring into the world

I believe in their worth

and I believe in mine

Isn't it funny...

Why is it that I love the unknown so much, I find myself leaping into it daily?
Why is it, that I run away from certainty?

Am I really a seeker of chaos and destruction?
What is it that I am truly looking for?
Who am I?

Questions without answers,
I do not know just yet what this mystery is all about

The mystical detective

You should know already,

how good of a detective I am,

I seek and seek

Like a mystic

In search for clues

As to who You are

Only to find You wherever I stand

My magical pen

My pen is a wand

My words are spells

My intentions are cast

Let the magic amass

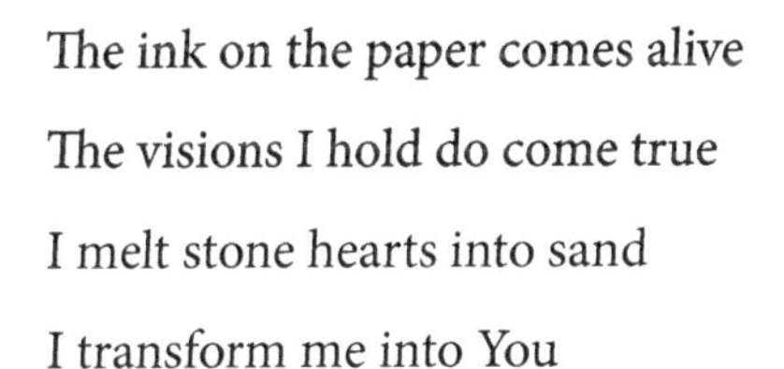

The ink on the paper comes alive

The visions I hold do come true

I melt stone hearts into sand

I transform me into You

I write what I want to see

I voice out loud what I want

I shape my reality

I am worthy of the life I want to live

I am deserving of love

I am all that I say I am

I am, that I am

And so, it is

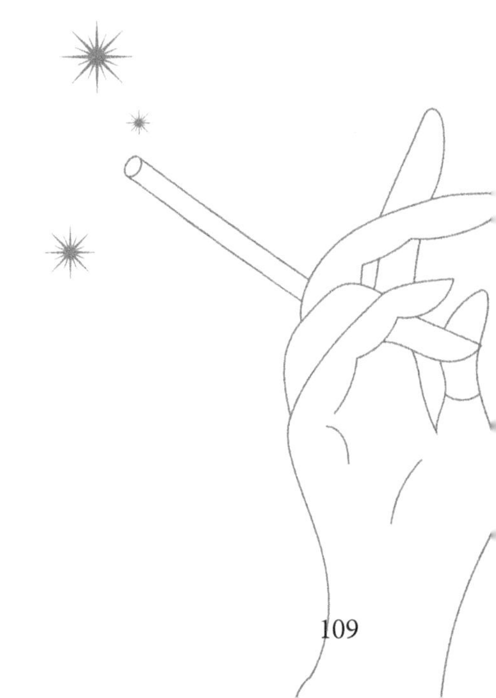

Grandmother's wisdom

I remembered today,
I remembered today the vision my grandmother had when she desired me
I remembered how I was just an idea before becoming a reality
I remembered how before I was born, I was simply a seed
A fragment of my grandmothers' imagination and dreams
I remembered today,
I remembered today the love my grandmother had before she held my mother in her hands
I also remembered the fear she had of losing and failing her
And then it hit me, like a lightning bolt,
How even the root of fear is love
Love has no beginning and no end and today,
I remembered that
again

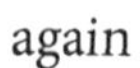

Father Sky

My father is like the extremes of the four seasons

When he is happy, he feels like a spring afternoon. He lights up the room and makes you feel like everything is possible

When he is angry, he feels like scorching heat underneath my feet

When he is stressed, he feels like a hurricane about to sweep my home apart

When he is cold, he is ice ice cold. Like the frozen pond we once took a dip in in Finland

Poetry is still alive

Is there still place for poetry in the world?
Everything seems to be so watered down
Our souls so tempered with.

Is there still space for me in this world?
Do you wonder about you too?
This washing out of your very essence becoming a stranger to your own kind.

This creeping feeling of needing to fit in, even though you'd rather not comply.
Fit into what exactly?

You think we would have outgrown these tiny, tiny boxes by now.

No, no, no I'd rather live in my world,
In my world, poetry is still the language of the soul,
Whispering daily:

"Look at the moon shining,
Look at the sea glistening,
Look at your father's wrinkles on his face.

Listen to the dices roll while the music is playing and your mother is complaining.

Listen closely to the wind blowing and feel it whipping against your face.

Touch the warm sand, plunge into the cold, cold waters.
Leave no rock unturned.

Send kisses to your angels daily.
Make a big deal out of being alive."

You can feel all of existence in one single moment.
With one simple breath.

You can feel it as long as you don't disguise, hide, or pretend.
Take up space, write your words, share your voice out loud, dance and be here.

Be here.
Be here.
Be here now.

Love looks good on you

Loosen your grip on life

How can you write your story if you are chocking it up?

Spending too much doubting yourself

Your powers

Comparing yourself to others

Loosen your grip

Allow life to drip through your fingers

Give it room to move

Do not hold on to your rigid ideas of how life should look like, or be like

Do not mould the unmouldable

Do not stop the unstoppable

Let life drip from your chin and your hair

Let love be the note you play

Make your body, a home body, a body of love

How do you know that the story you want to write is greater than the one that wants to be written?

Sweet soul of mine

The inner workings of my soul, led by a force greater than me
I surrender to it daily, believing it knows what is meant to be

The inner workings of my mind, gripping to stories from long ago,
I release expectations of where this mind of mine shall go

The inner workings of my body, living in the fears of yesterday,
worries of tomorrow,
I let go of the need to dance to a beat that is not my own

I release expectations of what I think ought to be mine and I choose daily to be in love with this sweet soul of mine

You are instrumental

I may not play any instruments, but I

I am an instrument

My heartstrings are like guitar strings

(crescendo)

My voice, a trumpet,

My body, a piano

Do, re, mi, fa, so, la, si,

No

(diminuendo)

Pianos are hard

And my body soft

Heart beating to the rhythm of nature

Notes of love moving beneath my skin

Orchestrating a melody written by the soul

I, vibrate on love

A sage is me

A sage once told me, to not look outside of myself

for the wisdom I seeked lived within

A sage once told me, to stop looking for answers in books

for the truth would come alive by living

A sage once told me, to never put anyone on a pedestal

for no one is higher or lower in the Kingdom of One

A sage once told me to be weary of those who painted themselves

as saints for everyone has sinned, yet not all have repented

A sage once told me to take a look at my reflection and to see

for that sage was me

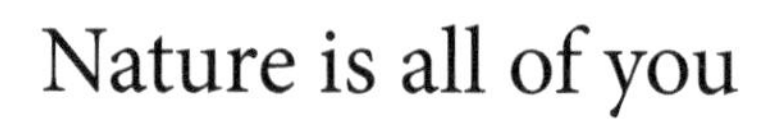

Nature is all of you

Nature doesn't apologise for her wild and neither should you.

Nature is both silent and noisy and so are you.

Nature is untamed.

Unconditioned.

Unfiltered.

She is both exquisite and messy.

Eternal and permanent.

The Source who created Nature also created you.

You are nature.

Nature is all of you

Mantras on peace

I feel most at peace when I do not force anything to happen

I feel most at ease when I allow things to unfold the way they should

I feel most in love when I surrender deeply to a God of my own understanding

I feel most at one when I see me in you, and you in me

The mystery of the heart

My heart is like an ocean
It is deep, it is vast and it has immeasurable power

My feelings are like waves that crash onto the shore, they come and they go
I have learned to not hold onto them for too long to not drown in my own sorrow

Occasionally, the power of my heart is so strong, it sends ripple effects into the world
Beautifying everything
Myself and others
It sends frequency of waves that are capable of cleansing the world, my world, healing everything on its way

My heart is like an ocean
It is dark, frightening and full of mystery

When it gets angry, it devastates the shores

It engulfs the world, my world with madness and chaos

It sends waves of insecurity and fear throughout my whole being

It breaks into a million grains of sand that was once part of a rock

And this is how I've come to understand that heart break is necessary for the heart to soften

How the shores can never be fully safe

How my heart is like an ocean and that light will only enter when it is broken

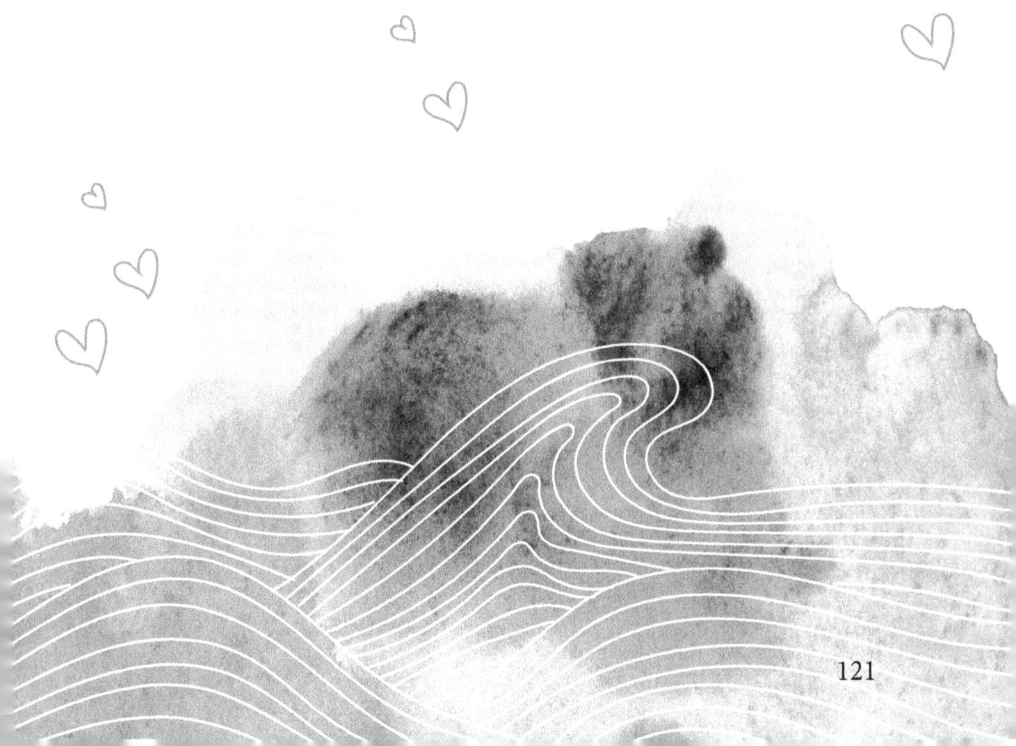

Transformation

Where there was confusion, let there be clarity

Where there was shame, let there be freedom

Where there was guilt, let there be gratitude

Where there was struggle, let there be ease

Where there was loss, remember it began with love

Dance through the storm

Can you dance with life during a storm?

Are you okay dancing in the rain with mud on your feet? Tangles in your hair?

Can you love life unconditionally even if life isn't returning your desires?

Can you love life simply because you are breathing and alive?

Do you have to have reasons to be dancing?

Dance, dance, dance

Regardless of what is happening

Life is happening for you right now; will you join it in eternity?

Moon drunk

Moon drunk from my sleep last night

I'm finding it harder to feel light

Shedding layers of my worn out skin

Is it true that I can always just begin?

Be reborn like a baby fresh out the womb

Have I outgrown my flesh and am I ready to bloom?

My shadows stopping me on my track

Constantly trying to pull me back

"Who do you think you are?" it keeps asking of me

"I'm a wave that has finally recognised it is the whole damn sea"

"I am the ocean, always in motion, no longer influenced by her wild emotions"

Peace is available to you now

Although there is wind at the surface and the waves are crashing against the shore,
Feel the calmness, like the still water at the deepest parts of the ocean.

Although there is wind and the leaves are shaking,
Feel rooted like the tallest and most grounded of trees.

Remember, your feet connect you to the depths of the Earth.
No external situation can uproot or unsteady you.

Your belly contains the sunlight of a million and one suns,
No amount of fire will ever damage or burn you.

Your body is made up of water,
Allow yourself to adapt and flow to all that surrounds you.

Your soul connects you to the sky above you,
Feel the air holding you always and you will never feel alone.

Let yourself dance to the rhythms of the Earth, Fire, Water and Air along the way.

Trust that everywhere you go, there is Spirit

Warmth

The light enters, I let it

It moves through me for a while, I allow it

It warms me up like a cozy blanket

Reassuring me I am right on time

I thank it

Yin and Yang

The dark flows and becomes the light

The light fades and becomes the dark

Life constantly moving between both ends of the spectrum

Never separated from one another

The two merged together, synced to their own rhythm

It resembles a dance between my shadow and I

The darkness

The light

Pulsing through you

Invite them both to stay

Coursing through your deepest of layers all the way in to

the depths of the mind

Forever balancing each other out

There is no darkness without light

No lightness without darkness

Bound together forever like molecules of water

One can never have one without the other

The cycle of life

An acorn becoming a tree

A tear making a sea

A seed burgeoning me

How can something so small be so grand

Grandeur there is

When I merge with the infinite and become one with all that exists

Reborn into an acorn becoming a tree once more

Be wild

Just let life be wild

As it is

Just let yourself be wild

As you are

Do not try to tame yourself

For a wilder, more uncontrollable beast shall appear

Do not hide your stories out of shame

Share them out of service

Out of love

Dream big

Many dreams, many wishes

I count my blessings each day

Instead of my curses

I get impatient when they don't just appear at the snap of my fingers

"You're taking too long" I scream out loud

"Patience is a virtue, my child

And so is your presence

Remember to play as though you already have it

What you ask for, has already been given

It is whether you are aware or not of your presents

It is whether you are aware or not of your magic"

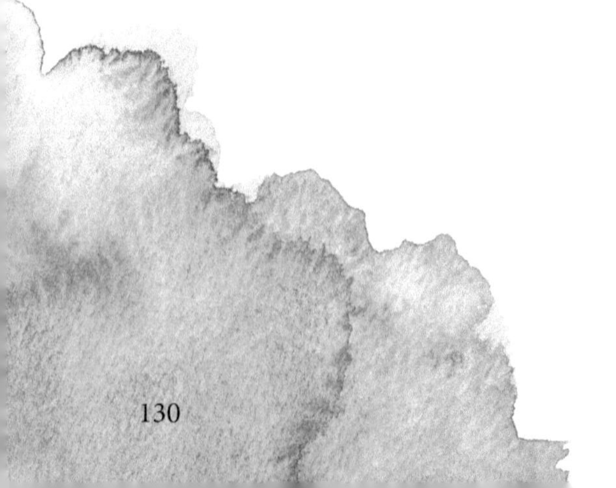

All a part of the dance

It is all a part of the dance

The panic, the anxiety, the confusion.

It is all a part of the dance.

The heartbreak, the grief, the disappointments.

It is all a part of the dance.

The connections, the detours, the love.

All of it.

It is all a part of the dance.

The songs may change.

The tempo may go up and down.

The beat, faster and slower.

Louder and quieter.

But the songs are always playing and you are always dancing.

You can choose to do so on your knees or on your feet.

With grace and ease.

With an open or closed heart.

You can do so with tears of sadness or laughter in your eyes.

It is all a part of the dance.

I believe ...

The moon holds secrets if we pay close attention

I believe ...

True love never dies

Inner peace is the real prize

Everything else is just poor disguise

I believe ...

The sea heals the soul

And we are always whole

I believe ...

Answers are found in silence

But those who love you will be verbal

I believe...

Life is eternal

And God's love is universal

So many connections to explore

Oh, do not implore

Or lament

Only

You must still find beauty in separation

Look at you, you are Me

In human form

Don't you want to see how we can perform?

"All the world's a stage"

As Shakespeare once wrote

I'm downing tea down my throat

Soothing my belly, making me merry

Forgetting you

You believe the remedy is in he

Or she

Or they

But hey, hey,

Look at you, look at your day

What is it that you do?

And how is it that you do it?

I am the weather

I cried of joy a moment ago

Now, the rain starts to fall

On a half sunny day

Me & the blues

No moon to blame tonight

For feeling the way I feel

No cosmic event today

For the turbulent energy inside

It's just me and the blues

Coming home to yourself feels like...

Accepting the present moment as it is, you as you are

A clear and open mind

An intimate dance with life

Coming home to yourself feels like...

Being light yet grounded

Living in alignment with your True Self

Freedom

Coming home to yourself feels like…

Forgiving myself and others

Letting go of the past

Loving God

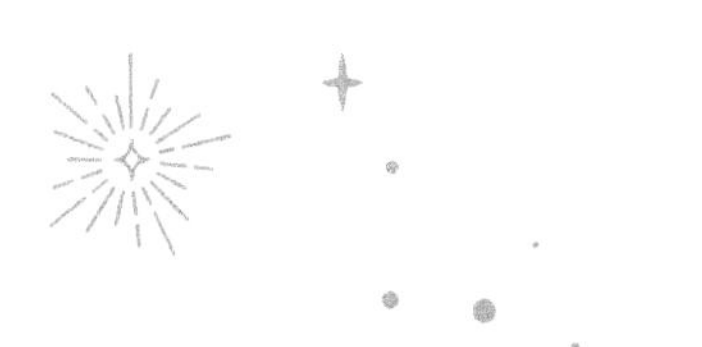

I am a mystic

I am a mystic who tried to be logical and mathematical instead of magnetic and magical

I am a mystic
Who knows before they know,
Because I feel it before it can be seen

I am a mystic who gazes into your soul to see the whirlwind happening within

I am a mystic who casts spells with every word I utter

I am a mystic who no longer shudders in fear, but in excitement as I stare at the world in pure wonder

I am a mystic who receives messages when the lights go out

I am a mystic who comes alive even without a glass of wine

Magical plant

I am her and she is me.

The old wise wild woman

and the talking tree.

Love is bigger

That?

That is not love.

That is tainted love.

That is love painted as loved.

Maybe even written as love.

But it is not love.

At least not love with a capital L.

At least not a divine, unified, coherent Love that is present at each moment of each day within everyone everywhere.

Plot twists

Oh, it gets a lot wilder.

The plot twists twistier.

You, become thirstier for a greater life.

A greater love.

A grandeur.

A candour.

You, become a troubadour.

Writing the story of your own life.

Dancing to the rhythm of your own heart beat.

Listening to your own goddamn voice.

Being an instrument for greatness.

Because the Universe is grand.

And you know exactly what to do.

And you're right on time to do it.

To release fear.

To trust the path.

Tonight under the moonlight

I made a claim tonight
As I looked directly at the moon light

"I do I do I do"
I trust in You
I trust in Your plan
More than I do in mine

"I do I do I do"
I relax in your hand,
It has been a while

Some time ago, I let go to journey on my own
Until I realised I had nowhere to go
Without You, nothing makes sense
Without You, it is a losing hand

You, who is always there
My true love, my only lover

"I do I do I do"
I trust in You
I trust in Your plan
More than I do in mine

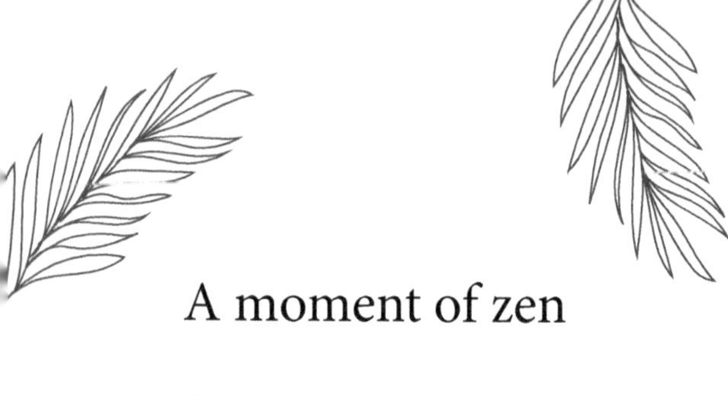

A moment of zen

Standing over the cliffs,

Overlooking the greenery,

The rocks

An easy feeling first arises,

The wind makes me feel at home,

And then, sneakily,

A second sensation makes its way through the cracks.

Fears,

Of losing a step,

Of crashing into a rock,

Of getting old alone,

Of being an ignorant,

Of not blooming in spring,

Of exploring again what should be forgotten,

An old lover rings the phone.

What if today is the day…

You choose to let go of an old belief or pattern that doesn't serve you
You fed your mind with good thoughts
You planted new seeds

What if today is the day…
You decided to no longer tear your body apart
You walked away from what disempowers you
You moved the way that Love wants you to move

What if today is the day…
You payed a bit more attention to your breath
and less attention to your limited beliefs

What if today you remembered your divinity, recognised your grace, reclaimed your power
What if today was always the day
The only day to believe in yourself again

Evolution

I will not go to my deathbed with words left unsaid

With love left unloved and unexplored

I will not go with sorrow

For who knows about a tomorrow?

Will I still be here?

And if so,

will I keep living

in fear?

Or will I finally come out of the shadows and stand in the light?

Oh, what a delight it would be when I finally come alive

To feast on all that deliciousness served from up above

Oh, what a sight it would be

To see,

my one true love

Oh, what might become of me

When I am

in

love,

I

Evolve

Things I am grateful for

The smell of fresh flowers and the sound of the birds

And the sight of light streaming through

And the taste of childhood on my tongue

And the feeling of fresh sheets on my skin

And the literal belly aches because my best friend is the funniest

And my mother walking through the door

Stay wild

You may appear wild to others who choose to follow the path

You may awaken those who are fast asleep and put them back on track

You may plant seeds in empty pots and grow gardens

You may not know your impact, yet know you impact everyone everywhere

Oh, how I dare you to not hold your tongue
To let the words roll out and say what you want

I dare you to stop fitting into things you've now outgrown

To let go of the past and walk into the unknown

The power of visualisation

What if…

You could embody who you want to be, before you become it?

You could live the life you want, before you lived it?

You could feel what you want to feel, before you experienced it?

You could live your dream life, before you even dreamt it?

What if cause didn't always precede effect?

What if the only thing you ever had to work on is your vibration?

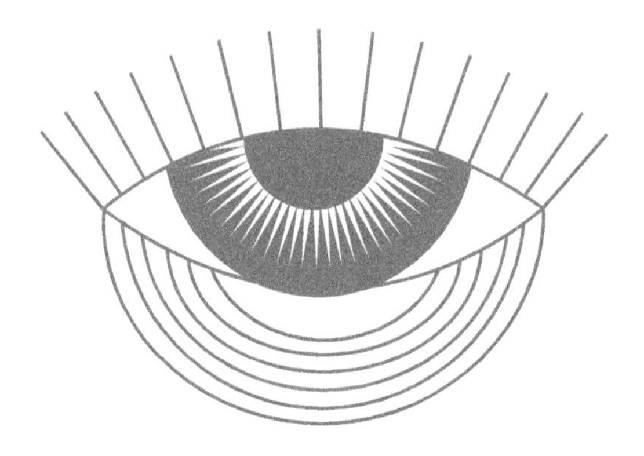

The circle of life

From no-thingness to a seed inside of a warm womb,

Life begins in darkness.

Feeling lost at first, you'll seek guidance from outside of yourself,

You'll be in the passenger seat,

Lost in a sea of other people's voices.

You'll forget you have the answers inside,

You'll forget you're complete, whole and worthy.

Until you remember again;

You are the love you are seeking for,

You are the medicine,

You are the Universe,

You are consciousness.

Become a child again, it is the only way to know God,

To believe, your heart must be untamed, fresh, and innocent,

Life will keep spinning and with it your head too,
As it tries to cling to what has been,
Let go, lose yourself,
Change is the only constant.

When you feel fear, soothe yourself with the truth that everyone is just a projection of your own mind and experiences,
No one can harm you.

Celebrate,
Dance in the rain, surround yourself with good company.

Let go of the guilt you feel,
The shame, the unworthiness, the split mind,
Allow yourself to feel blissful, to love life,
It is your divine right,

Remember,
Be a fool,
Keep your heart open to love,
Love fully, no matter the amount of heartbreaks,

You'll get ripe with time,

You'll age like fine wine,

You'll bloom,

You'll ride the wave of success ,

Soar to new heights,

Beam,

But not without trials and lessons, grief and heartbreak.

All of life happens while making your way back to no-thingness,

Back to a seed,

Inside of a warm womb.

Life is not a mystery to be solved

I keep asking myself

Do I stay?

Do I leave?

What if I make a mistake?

Experience, child

Experience life

Experience the moment

Experience the feeling

Experience the thought

Listen, child

Listen to your inner voice

Listen to the whispers of your heart

Listen to your gut feeling

Listen to your own intuition

Life is not a mystery to be solved

Life is a mystery to be lived

Magnetism

May you know this about yourself,

You are magnetic

Magic

Magnificent

(Me)dicine

Do not make anyone or anything but yourself the remedy

or the cure

You are your own medicine

LOVE

ROMANCE IS NOT DEAD

In the space of my heart lies many chambers,

Rooms I have visited,

And some I have yet to discover.

In the space of my heart, I still have an ache remaining,

An ache for things I cannot explain,

It goes something like this:

"Don't be afraid to love again.

To put all your cards on the table.

Don't fear loving.

Don't fear being loved.

You cannot be rejected, only drawn closer to your beloved.

It does exist.

It does transform.

It heals.

It is healing.

This love is a deep love of acceptance and creation.

Of union. Of mysticism. Of wildness.

It does exist.

There is no separation.

It is always One."

Romance is not a fairy tale

I have decided to write again. Write what?

Ah, I don't know!

A book?

Poetry?

I'll write it on love and deception.

No, no,

On love and betrayal!

Wait, maybe,

I'll start here.

Once upon a time,

Disney movies fucked us all up.

My first love?

Life itself

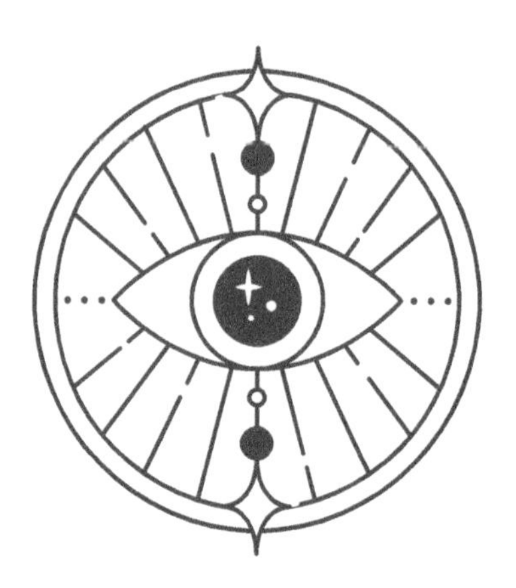

My second, self-love

Through the eyes of a guy,

I might seem a little bit shy

Don't come too close, you might lose an eye

With a fortress built around my heart

I have saved it only for One

Myself

A lot of times we settle

A lot of times, we settle

We settle for a love that does not feel like love

Because we are unaware of what it feels like to truly love ourselves

A lot of times, we settle

We settle for a life that does not make us feel alive

Because we are afraid that living fully is a step closer to death

A lot of times, we settle

We settle for a truth, that does not feel like the truth to cover up the lie we choose to show to the world

A lot of times, we settle

We settle for the comfort, the momentarily pleasures and happiness, terrified of what the unknown has in store for us

We settle for safe, for the minimum because we are oblivious of the safety that life provides even in despair and isolation

So, do not settle

Do not settle for a love less than,

A life less than grand

Do not settle for the minimum,

Do not settle for lies and deceit

Settle for honesty, purity, compassion

Settle for kindness

Settle for authenticity

Settle for the discomfort that life brings when you step into unchartered territories

Twin flames

A time before our time,

A soul split into two

One heart that used to beat as one

Now beating to the sound of two

One mind that used to think as one

Now thinking to the thoughts of two

One body once glued together

Now moving to the rhythm of two

Living through hundreds of lives on their own

They travelled the world apart

Drifting further to chart

Their own way

One fateful day, their paths crossed again

Cut from the same cloth,

They were like moths to a flame

Joined at the hips, their arms always intertwined

Like we need gravity to be

They needed each other to breathe

But they knew

They knew they would be walking through fire

Used to being two,

They no longer knew

how to be

One again

Into the wild

Born in the wild, I know my way

Into the wild, I go each day

Run with the wild, I fall to my knees and pray

"Keep me fierce, but gentle. Keep me strong, but nimble. Keep me loved, but free."

Born in the wild, I need no map to find you

Into the wild, everything becomes anew,

Run with the wild, breathing is a breakthrough

Wild I am, and wild are you

Wandering through the jungle

Together, yet apart,

Paving our own routes, wondering if we will drift or make art?

Let me be drunk

I wanted to be drunk and lose my head

I wanted to twirl around and feel alive instead of dead

I wanted to fly to new heights and spread across the sky

And yet,

Forecasting too far ahead

You sobered me up faster than ice cold water

Ending the book before the chapter even ran

The Sea Kissing the Shore

We talked and talked until the middle of the night
Phones glued to our hands
How good it felt to reunite

For a brief moment, it felt like the sea kissing the shore
Smooth, soft and steady

It was too hard to ignore
The streams of emotions flooding my body

I was sure I would not drown
For I knew how to swim
I was counting on our lucky stars
For us to not go on a whim

But the moon changed shape and so did you
High tide, low tide,
I could no longer endure

The sea stopped kissing the shore

And we let go of each other's hands

Oh, a physical rapture has taken place

But I ponder, if what we had could ever be replaced?

Could the sea ever stop kissing the shore?

Sorry mom and dad

More than a booty call

Less than a girlfriend

Our love story was a whirlwind

He wants to have his cake and eat me too

Freedom seems to be at the tip of his tongue

Freedom is all that he craves

More than a booty call

Less than a girlfriend

Our love story was a whirlwind

He wears his heart on his sleeve when his shirt is on

But where is his heart when the clothes come off?

More than a booty call

Less than a girlfriend

Our love story was a whirlwind

What is a man to do when he desires freedom and you?

A partnership would sink his ship,

But little does he know, a life without you would too

Waiting and Waiting

Phone in my hands

Head turned down

I miss the sunset

I miss the rain

Phone in my hands

Head turned down

Expecting something to happen

Hoping for someone to reach out

The phone rings

It's not you

It's not now

I will not be waiting forever

Another greater one is around the corner

My fire burns stronger apart, anyway

When you call my name

I'm sensing a shift in your voice

A change in how I feel when your name pops up on my screen

It's not the same

When you call my name

The butterflies escaped from their cage

My heart no longer skips a beat

I can now take the heat

When my father shouts

I no longer cry

Let them eat cake!

I want to have my cake and eat it too

I want it all, just like you

Unsatisfied with crumbs

I left you and became numb

Oh, just for a little while

It felt like forever

But I, I was finally eating my cake and enjoying the weather

The revolution

He was looking outside the window

As he watched the love of his life walk away

Undisturbed, she was

Walking down the streets revolting

Making the voices of those unheard, heard again

She wanted to be loud after being quiet for so long

She wanted to make some noise, some real noise

She wanted to shake things up, him up

She herself knew

This was the wrong time for this story to unfold

She wanted it all and this was not it, at all

But how do you give up on something that feels good?

How do you give up that high?

Oh, oh, the ecstasy

Beware of it

Especially when you find it in another person

Deadlock

I'm at a deadlock
A standstill

My heart belongs to you
Chained to the desires of you

Trying to lift my legs and walk away
Run away
But how?

Every time I move, I fall
Flat on my face

I'm stuck in a quicksand
The earth is thickening
Swallowing me up

I wake up with the words deadlock on my mouth

An image of two swords touching floating in my head

They're at a deadlock

A standstill

Unrelenting

Uncompromising

I want to lay down my arms and go back to sleep instead

I'm tired

I no longer want to keep fighting for us, not even in my dreams

Mindfield

My mind is a minefield
A "no you" zone
Ready to shut down and kill
Any thoughts of us ever being together

Sometimes,
I purposely miss it
I think about us building a life, a home,
Having children
For a split second
I don't want to destroy it all to the ground

Oh, a split second,
A second personality arises
I don't want to do this to myself

My mind is a minefield
A "no you" zone
Ready to shut down and kill
Any thoughts of us ever being together

I have a guard now

Watching and monitoring more closely

Any thought that resembles you gets thrown out

I shut it down

I shut it down

I'm a serial killer now

A serial killer!

I kill every thought about us that walks through my mind

Bang!

Bang!

Bye,

Bye,

The thought is gone now,

But are you?

And for how long?

It's still pitch black

It's still pitch black
It's still pitch black
While I await for you to come back

Where have you gone and why?
Did we just let true love pass by?

Even though I still feel sore
I await your return no more

Shortly, the sun will pierce through the dark skies
Light will come through
Light will come through
It most certainly has to

But night life exists somewhere at any point
Just as you'll walk through my mind at some point

It's still pitch black somewhere in the world as the sun rises where I stand

Light has come through here
And now, there is less fear
Love is not just an affair
Love is not just there

It is already here
Like the crack of dawn
My definition of love has grown
As I have now become my own
And made my home, the unknown

Our love is not a Disney fairy tale

I had a scare

Was our time together real, a dream or a nightmare?

Trying to paint a painting of what it was

My dreams now have turned to dust

You lost my trust and everything went bust

The colors I'd use now are different

The poems I'll write will change

You'll no longer be the main character of the story

I'm taking back all of the glory

I'm planting the crown back on my head and looking ahead

For I am a Queen who pledges allegiance to no one

Not a knight, nor a king

A prince or a pauper

This is no Disney fairy tale

I choose me as it always should be

One of us has to, and it certainly wasn't you, was it?

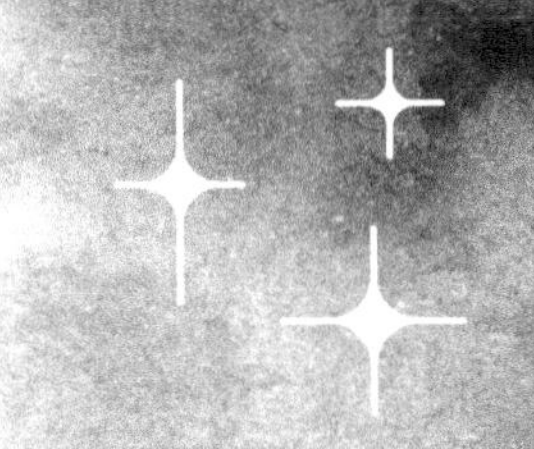

What will happen when we meet again?

And when we meet again,
How will I greet you when you ring the bell?

Will you tell me of your new conquests and discoveries?
Will you share your new tales and memories?

Will I still have a small place in your heart?
And will I still make an appearance in your art?

A love story that never got to be all that it could be,
Was it worth it to you to have but only a piece of me?

Oasis

I walked through the desert for some time

Seeking refuge in the scorching heat

Sand dunes below my feet

Gentle warm breeze blowing my hair

I was looking for water to quench my thirst

But instead, here it was that you emerged

Like a mirage, I found you instead

Oh, how wrong I was for thinking this love story was dead

Having wandered the desert for some time

You too were in search of water

Seeking refuge in the scorching heat

You were burning with fire and desire

Your insides were just as hot as the blazing sun burning my skin

Burning me from within

The heat made us both sleepy and we fell asleep in each other's arms

On the bed of sand below our bodies

Moonlight and stars

Shooting above our hazy heads

We woke up from our slumber in a daze

When the sun rose over our sandy face

It was not long after that thunder stroke and the sky magically broke

Rain mixed with earth, wind and fire

Something out of the ordinary was about to transpire

A treasure appeared right in front of my eyes

It was me standing without my disguise

I suddenly remembered what was missing

Surrender was always the greatest blessing

You, were just a mirage for the blind

For True love was faceless,

Nameless,

Painless

You got cold hands

We already tried it out and the fire burned out
What is there more to find?
That our energies intertwine?
That our love ages like fine wine?

That we make more sense in real life,
Than we do on paper?

That life seems to have other plans in store for us
Fooling us into believing we could work it out?

As though we ever stood a chance at being grand together,
What is there more to find out that we have not?

That our pieces fit so well together?
That our bodies move as one?
That our breath stops as we kiss?

I don't know where I and you, end and begin

I don't know how,
Time seems to stop when you take my hand and brush the hair

Out of my face

I don't know where this love goes when you walk out the door in the morning

You bring heaven to hell

And hell is when you walk away the very next day

We already tried it out and the fire burned out,

What is there more to find?

That our energies intertwine?

That our love ages like fine wine?

Life seems to have other plans in store for us

And it does not seem to include the two of us,

Together

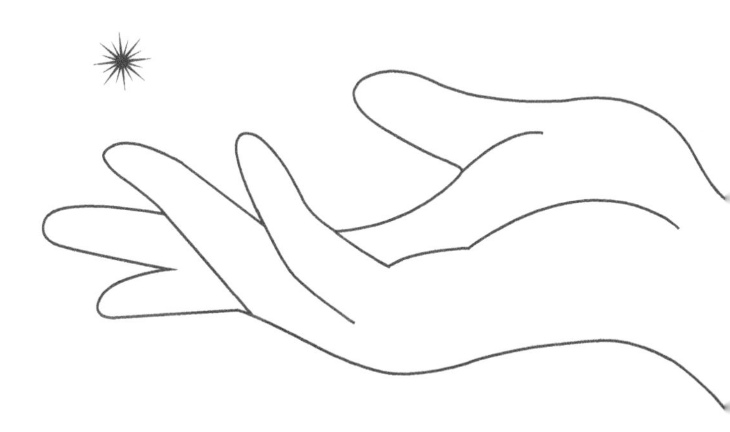

Mystical love

I look for you in crowds I know I will not see your face

I wait to find your scent again in places I know you haven't been to

I close my eyes, it's better
For at least there,
I can hold you in my third eye centre

My heart beats differently now that you've made your mark on it

Some people come into your life
Like a storm,
Sweep you off your feet,
And then,
Leave you dancing alone

Oh, it seems like the worst,
Dancing alone,
But the real crime would be,
Not to dance
At all

Extremes

I left you in the cold so you would know

What it feels like to be frozen

Isolated from your love, I did not feel chosen

Deprived from your love, I felt a bit broken

I wandered through the desert with one lover, only to end up

walking on ice with you

Well, it seems

I must be good at tolerating extremes

Two wandering travellers

Across space and time,

Two wandering travellers meet

Just for a little while, just for the time being

They lock eyes, with a soulful gaze

They shared stories at first,

Of their birth and past lives,

Of their thirst and desires

She wanted to know all of him

He wanted to know all of her

Across space and time,

Two wandering travellers meet

She, wild and tamed,

Wanting to undress his mind and appease his soul

He, determined and relentless

Desiring to unzip her dress, to stare at her nakedness

All she wants is for him to claim her

All he wants is for some company on his journey home

But as wandering travellers always do, they parted ways

In the most amicable of ways

No revenge nor resentment

No regret nor torments

Ancient Times

Your ancient hands on my ancient soul is now ancient history,
Like a dinosaur fossil sitting in a museum
The end of a chapter from a dusty old book
You were a stepping stone from the old ages
To remind me of my greatness

I rise above the physical need to desire you,
I ascend
I ascend
Higher and higher
More bold
More powerful
I become

Your hands were like chains keeping me down
Underground in the dark
Unpredictable and electric
Undeserving of my sacredness

Your ancient hands on my ancient soul is now ancient history
But I've been told, history repeats itself

Exceptional men

I have known exceptional men

Exceptionally deceiving

Deceitful

Disturbing

Disturbed

Delusional

Delirious

Delicious

Distinguished

Disgusting

Driven

Dry

Dumb

Drunk

Devoted

Domestic

Deep

Growing pains

Oh, but did you think you would ever stop growing through love and heartbreak?

Power Trip

We were both in our power trips

Refusing to let love in the way love wants to come in

But love,

Love has its ways,

It weaves through and cracks through

It removes barriers

Burns down bridges

Builds new ones

Oh, when love wants to come through

It comes through

Unknots

Unbinds

It is

Unreal

Unstoppable

Monumental disaster

I had a lover once who wrote poetry about me
As though I was the statue of liberty
His words on paper were a symphony
A melody
A love language I could finally understand
It moved me fiercely
Cut me deeply

What are words but an interpretation of our vision?
An incompleteness of the truth
A distortion of reality
A battle of the egos
Ephemeral just like us
Fleeting as quickly as they come in

You can be a monument to a lover one day
And ten feet underground the very next

A living dead in his head
Very much alive in space

Ghosts of the past

Seems like just the other day

We saw each other again

Your face, white as sheets

I no longer felt any heat

No, I am not a ghost

No not yet

I have not risen from the dead

You may have murdered me in your head

Buried me deep down in your psyche

Oh, you longed for me to disappear

You cut the scene, cut me off, cut me out

Bled me out

And yet, my head popped out

In front of you, out of the blue

If I were wild, I would have told you:

I am not upset with you, I thank you

You do not haunt my dreams

You are no longer a part of

I have not painted you as a villain but a foolish old lover

And yes, I dated your best friend, but you and I were long over

Everything and nothing changes

The bed you once shared laughs in, becomes the bed you feel shattered in

The floor your feet swept on while dancing, becomes the floor you weep on

The man you once knew and loved, changed faces too
You became all blue
After his departure
No longer able to breathe through the rapture

The objects did not change
But their significance did
The man did not grow
But you did

The sky changed within seconds,
But how about you?
Are you still trying to make sense of yesterday?
Are you not trying to live yet another day?

Thank you, next

Thank you for feeling so free to leave me when you did

I got closer to God almost immediately

True Love never dies

I leave before I am left

Out of fear of being abandoned or rejected

I let go of you before you even have the chance to

I cannot take yet another person leaving me, no not by choice at least

I'd rather be a fool and leave you first

Then have doubts in my mind about whether I quench your thirst

Where did I learn this?

Where does this pattern come from?

From long ago

There is still deep, deep sorrow

Lingering in me

Mystified, stupefied you play your old tricks on me

Again and again, I fall into them

Will I ever learn?

To be whole on my own

To not seek for what I already have

To be watchful when it all comes crumbling down

Free falling into love as my heart breaks open once more

With each and every rapture, I end up with more laughter

Your departure is not a disaster

You were never my forever after

Just simply a stop on my way as I become the master of my own destiny

And once again rediscover my divinity in a whole new way

Love your shadows

Love,

Love who you are

Love who you are fiercely

Then, extend that love to others

Love,

Love the way you do things

Love the way you work

Love the way you talk

Walk

Bark

Yes, you must also love the way you get angry

And the way you deal with conflict

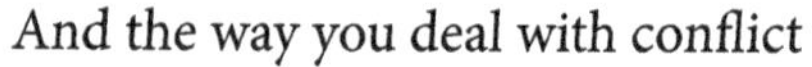

Love is...

Love is like taking a deep breath after turbulent times and feeling at home once more

Love is letting go of the idea of separation and the acknowledgment of oneness

Love is the discovery of God in each and every moment

Love is forgiving yourself and others, as many times as needed

Love is a calming balm on unhealed wounds

Love is sharing your authentic self with the world
Love is dropping the masks you have worn for far too long out of fear of being seen, rejected or abandoned

Love is like warm tears cooling down your face, untangling your heart

Love is realizing you are nothing less but divine

Love is treating yourself and your desires as sacred
Love is not looking away from your pain, but tending to it

Love is a reclamation of the present moment

Milton Keynes UK
Ingram Content Group UK Ltd.
UKHW020514210923
429022UK00010B/50